Engineering a Self-Sufficient Future: Strategies for Energy Independence in the United States

Copyright Page

TITLE: Engineering a Self-Sufficient Future: Strategies for Energy Independence in the United States

1ST Edition

Copyright @ 2023

ISBN: 9798223854135

Engineering a Self-Sufficient Future: Strategies for Energy Independence in the United States

By Roberto Miguel Rodriguez

Strategies for the United States to Become Self-Sufficient in Energy, Including Oil

Developing domestic solar power infrastructure

In recent years, the importance of renewable energy sources has become increasingly evident. As the world faces the challenges of climate change and the depletion of fossil fuels, engineers play a vital role in developing strategies for energy independence. One such strategy is the development of domestic solar power infrastructure.

Solar power is a clean, abundant, and renewable energy source that has the potential to transform the way we generate electricity. By harnessing the power of the sun, we can reduce our dependence on fossil fuels and decrease harmful greenhouse gas emissions. However, to fully realize the potential of solar energy, it is crucial to develop a robust domestic infrastructure.

Developing domestic solar power infrastructure involves several key aspects. Firstly, it requires the installation of solar panels on a large scale. Engineers must design and implement solar farms, rooftop installations, and other solar projects to maximize energy generation. This includes identifying suitable locations, optimizing panel placement, and ensuring efficient operation and maintenance.

Secondly, engineers must focus on improving solar energy storage capabilities. While solar energy is abundant during the day, it is not always available when needed, such as during peak demand hours or at night. Developing advanced battery technologies and energy storage systems is essential to overcome this challenge. Engineers can explore various options, including lithium-ion batteries, flow batteries, and thermal energy storage, to ensure a reliable and uninterrupted supply of solar power.

Furthermore, integrating solar power into the existing grid infrastructure is a critical aspect of its development. Engineers must work closely with utility companies to ensure smooth integration and grid stability. This involves designing smart grids, implementing advanced monitoring and control systems, and addressing any technical challenges that arise during the integration process.

To accelerate the development of domestic solar power infrastructure, engineers must also focus on research and development. Investing in cutting-edge technologies, such as thin-film solar panels, concentrated solar power, and solar thermal systems, can significantly improve the efficiency and cost-effectiveness of solar energy generation.

In conclusion, developing domestic solar power infrastructure is crucial for the United States to become self-sufficient in energy and reduce its dependence on foreign oil imports. Engineers play a pivotal role in designing, implementing, and optimizing solar projects, improving energy storage capabilities, integrating solar power into the grid, and advancing solar technologies through research and development. By harnessing the power of the sun, we can pave the way for a sustainable and self-sufficient future.

Benefits of solar energy

Solar energy is a rapidly growing field within the renewable energy sector, offering numerous benefits for engineers and the United States as a whole. With the goal of achieving energy independence, it is crucial to understand the advantages of solar energy and its potential impact on the country's future.

One of the key benefits of solar energy is its unlimited availability. The sun is an abundant and inexhaustible source of energy, providing a virtually limitless supply of power. Unlike fossil fuels, which are finite and subject to price volatility, solar energy offers a stable and predictable source of electricity. This reliability makes it an attractive option for engineers looking to design and develop sustainable energy systems.

Another advantage of solar energy is its environmental friendliness. Solar power generates electricity without producing harmful greenhouse gas emissions or air pollutants. By harnessing the sun's energy, engineers can contribute to reducing the United States' carbon footprint and combatting climate change. This aligns with the goal of developing renewable energy strategies and reducing dependence on foreign oil imports.

Solar energy also offers economic benefits. As the technology continues to advance, the cost of solar panels and installation has significantly decreased. This has made solar energy more accessible and affordable for individuals, businesses, and governments. Engineers can play a crucial role in developing domestic solar power infrastructure, creating jobs, and stimulating economic growth in the renewable energy sector.

Furthermore, solar energy provides energy security. By increasing the United States' reliance on domestically produced solar power, the country can reduce its vulnerability to geopolitical tensions and fluctuations in global energy markets. Investing in renewable energy sources, such as solar power, mitigates the risks associated with dependence on imported oil.

In conclusion, solar energy offers numerous benefits for engineers and the United States as a whole. From its unlimited availability and environmental friendliness to its economic advantages and contribution to energy security, solar energy plays a vital role in achieving energy independence. Engineers can contribute to this goal by developing domestic solar power infrastructure, implementing energy efficiency measures, and advancing research and development in alternative energy sources. By embracing solar energy, the United States can pave the way towards a self-sufficient future in energy.

Challenges in implementing solar power infrastructure

The implementation of solar power infrastructure has gained significant attention in recent years as the world strives to transition to a more sustainable and renewable energy future. However, despite its numerous benefits, there are several challenges that engineers face when it comes to implementing solar power infrastructure.

One of the primary challenges is the high initial cost associated with setting up solar power infrastructure. The cost of solar panels, inverters, batteries, and other necessary equipment can be prohibitive, especially for small-scale projects or individuals. Additionally, the installation and maintenance costs can further add to the overall expenses, making it difficult for many to invest in solar power infrastructure.

Another challenge is the intermittent nature of solar power. Unlike traditional sources of energy, such as coal or natural gas, solar power production is dependent on weather conditions and the availability of sunlight. This intermittency can lead to fluctuations in energy output, making it challenging to meet the consistent energy demands of consumers and businesses.

The integration of solar power infrastructure into existing electricity grids is also a significant challenge. The variability of solar power production requires careful coordination and management to ensure a stable and reliable power supply. This often requires the use of advanced technologies, such as energy storage systems and demand response mechanisms, to balance the supply and demand of electricity effectively.

Furthermore, the limited availability of suitable land for solar power installations poses a challenge. Solar farms require vast tracts of land, which may not always be readily available or suitable for development. Additionally, the environmental impact of large-scale solar installations, such as habitat disruption and land degradation, must be carefully considered and mitigated.

Another challenge is the lack of standardized regulations and policies regarding solar power infrastructure. Different states and local jurisdictions may have varying rules and incentives, creating a complex landscape for engineers to navigate. Streamlining regulations and establishing consistent policies can help promote the widespread adoption of solar power infrastructure across the United States.

In conclusion, while solar power infrastructure offers a promising solution for achieving energy independence and reducing reliance on fossil fuels, there are several challenges that engineers must overcome. These challenges range from the high initial cost and intermittency of solar power to the integration into existing grids and the availability of suitable land. However, with continued technological advancements and policy support, engineers can address these challenges and pave the way for a more sustainable and self-sufficient future powered by solar energy.

Strategies for increasing solar energy production

Solar energy is a key component in the pursuit of energy independence in the United States. As engineers, it is our responsibility to develop strategies that will maximize solar energy production and contribute to our goal of becoming self-sufficient in energy. This subchapter will explore various strategies that can be implemented to increase solar energy production and utilization in the United States.

One of the most effective strategies for increasing solar energy production is developing domestic solar power infrastructure. This involves investing in the construction of solar farms and rooftop solar installations across the country. By utilizing unused land and rooftops, we can harness the power of the sun and generate renewable energy on a large scale.

In addition to developing infrastructure, it is crucial to invest in research and development in solar energy technologies. This includes advancements in solar panel efficiency, energy storage systems, and grid integration. By improving the efficiency and reliability of solar energy systems, we can increase the overall production and utilization of solar energy in the United States.

To further encourage the adoption of solar energy, it is important to implement policies that reduce dependence on foreign oil imports. By providing incentives such as tax credits and subsidies for solar energy projects, we can make it more financially feasible for individuals and businesses to invest in solar power. Additionally, implementing net metering policies will allow individuals to sell excess solar energy back to the grid, further incentivizing the adoption of solar energy.

Another strategy for increasing solar energy production is promoting energy efficiency and conservation measures. By reducing energy consumption through energy-efficient buildings, appliances, and transportation, we can decrease the overall demand for energy and rely more heavily on renewable sources like solar power.

Furthermore, advancing solar technology in conjunction with other renewable energy sources such as wind, hydroelectric, and biofuels can create a more robust and reliable energy system. By integrating these sources into a smart grid, we can ensure a stable and efficient energy supply while reducing our dependence on fossil fuels.

In conclusion, increasing solar energy production is vital in achieving energy independence in the United States. By developing domestic solar power infrastructure, investing in research and development, implementing supportive policies, promoting energy efficiency, and integrating solar power with other renewable sources, we can maximize solar energy production and move closer to a self-sufficient future. As engineers, it is our duty to lead the charge in developing and implementing these strategies and pave the way for a cleaner and more sustainable energy landscape.

Integrating solar power into the national grid

Solar power has emerged as a promising solution to address the growing energy demands of the United States. As engineers, it is crucial for us to explore and implement strategies that integrate solar power into the national grid, paving the way for a self-sufficient future in energy.

Developing a robust domestic solar power infrastructure is an imperative step towards achieving energy independence. By focusing on the expansion of solar power generation, the United States can reduce its reliance on fossil fuels, decrease greenhouse gas emissions, and mitigate the effects of climate change. This can be accomplished through the installation of solar photovoltaic (PV) systems on rooftops, solar farms, and other suitable locations across the country.

To maximize the utilization of solar energy, it is vital to invest in the development of advanced technologies that enhance the efficiency and storage capacity of solar panels. This includes research and development in areas such as thin-film solar cells, concentrating solar power systems, and innovative energy storage solutions. By making solar power more affordable and efficient, we can encourage its widespread adoption and integration into the national grid.

In parallel, increasing wind energy production and utilization can complement the integration of solar power into the grid. Wind turbines can operate in tandem with solar panels, providing a consistent and reliable renewable energy supply. By strategically placing wind farms in areas with high wind resources, we can optimize the output of wind energy and further reduce dependence on fossil fuels.

Furthermore, investing in biofuel technologies can diversify our energy sources and reduce the environmental impact associated with traditional transportation fuels. Biofuels, such as ethanol and biodiesel, can be produced from organic materials, including agricultural crops and waste products. By promoting the development of biofuel production facilities, we can support local economies, reduce greenhouse gas emissions, and decrease our reliance on imported oil.

In conclusion, integrating solar power into the national grid is a crucial step towards achieving energy independence in the United States. By developing domestic solar power infrastructure, increasing wind energy production, investing in biofuel technologies, and implementing conservation measures, engineers can contribute to a self-sufficient future in energy. Through strategic planning, policy implementation, and technological advancements, we can reduce our dependence on foreign oil imports, mitigate climate change, and create a sustainable energy landscape for future generations.

Increasing wind energy production and utilization

Wind energy is one of the most promising renewable energy sources in the pursuit of energy independence in the United States. As engineers, it is our responsibility to explore and implement strategies to increase the production and utilization of wind energy. This subchapter will delve into the potential of wind energy, the challenges it faces, and the strategies we can employ to maximize its contribution to our self-sufficiency goals.

Wind energy has gained significant traction in recent years due to its numerous advantages. It is clean, abundant, and widely distributed, making it a viable option for regions across the country. Additionally, wind power has the potential to reduce greenhouse gas emissions and decrease our dependence on fossil fuels. However, there are certain challenges that need to be addressed to fully harness its potential.

One of the key challenges in wind energy production is intermittency. Wind is not constant, and its availability fluctuates. Engineers must work to develop advanced forecasting models and energy storage systems to mitigate the effects of intermittency. Additionally, there is a need for further research and development in wind turbine technology to improve efficiency and reduce costs.

To increase wind energy production, we must identify suitable locations for wind farms. This requires comprehensive mapping and analysis of wind resources across the country. Engineers can leverage advanced data analytics and machine learning algorithms to identify the most optimal sites for wind farms. Moreover, collaboration with local communities is crucial to ensure that wind farms are developed in harmony with the environment and do not disrupt the lives of nearby residents.

Utilization of wind energy can be enhanced by expanding the transmission infrastructure. Engineers can design and implement a robust grid system that can efficiently transmit wind-generated electricity across states. This would enable the transfer of surplus wind power from regions with excess generation capacity to areas with higher demand.

Furthermore, engineers should focus on integrating wind energy with other renewable energy sources. By combining wind power with solar, hydroelectric, and geothermal energy, we can create a diversified and reliable energy mix. This would also help address the issue of intermittency and provide a more stable and consistent power supply.

In conclusion, increasing wind energy production and utilization is crucial in our journey towards energy independence. As engineers, we must embrace innovation and collaboration to overcome the challenges associated with wind power. By implementing advanced technologies, optimizing wind farm locations, expanding transmission infrastructure, and integrating different renewable energy sources, we can maximize the potential of wind energy and contribute significantly to our self-sufficiency goals.

Advantages of wind energy

Wind energy is a powerful and renewable source of energy that has numerous advantages for the United States as it strives for energy independence. This subchapter explores the various benefits of harnessing wind power and highlights its potential to contribute to a self-sufficient energy future.

One of the key advantages of wind energy is its environmental friendliness. Unlike fossil fuels, wind power produces zero greenhouse gas emissions, meaning it does not contribute to climate change. By investing in wind energy, the United States can significantly reduce its carbon footprint and mitigate the effects of global warming. Furthermore, wind turbines have a minimal land footprint, allowing for the coexistence of wind farms and other land uses, such as agriculture.

Another advantage of wind energy is its abundant availability. The United States has vast wind resources, particularly in the Midwest and along the coasts, making it an ideal candidate for wind power expansion. By increasing wind energy production and utilization, the country can tap into this vast resource and decrease its reliance on imported energy sources.

Wind energy also offers economic benefits. The construction and maintenance of wind farms create job opportunities, stimulating local economies. Additionally, wind power provides a stable and predictable energy source, which can help reduce electricity price volatility and enhance energy security.

In terms of energy diversification, wind power plays a crucial role in reducing dependence on foreign oil imports. By investing in domestic wind energy infrastructure, the United States can decrease its reliance on unstable oil-producing regions and enhance energy independence.

Furthermore, wind energy is a flexible and scalable source of power. It can be utilized in various applications, from small-scale residential installations to large-scale utility projects. This versatility allows for the integration of wind power into existing energy systems without significant disruptions.

To fully realize the advantages of wind energy, continued research and development are necessary. Engineers play a vital role in advancing wind turbine technology, improving efficiency, and reducing costs. By encouraging research and development in alternative energy sources like wind power, the United States can accelerate its transition towards a self-sufficient energy future.

In conclusion, wind energy offers numerous advantages for the United States as it strives for energy independence. Its environmental friendliness, abundant availability, economic benefits, energy diversification, and scalability make it a crucial component of a self-sufficient energy strategy. By increasing wind energy production and utilization, investing in wind infrastructure, and fostering research and development, engineers can contribute to a sustainable and self-reliant energy future for the United States.

Overcoming challenges in wind energy production
Introduction:

Wind energy has emerged as a key player in the pursuit of energy independence and sustainability. Harnessing the power of the wind to generate electricity has become increasingly important as the United States seeks to reduce its dependence on fossil fuels and foreign oil imports. However, like any other energy source, wind energy production comes with its own set of challenges. This subchapter explores some of the obstacles faced in wind energy production and provides strategies for engineers to overcome them.

1. Grid Integration:

One of the primary challenges in wind energy production is integrating the generated electricity into the existing power grid. The intermittent nature of wind power requires a robust and flexible grid that can handle fluctuations in supply and demand. Engineers must work on developing advanced grid management systems that can effectively balance the variability of wind energy with other sources.

2. Storage Solutions:

Another challenge is storing excess wind energy for times when the wind is not blowing. Engineers should focus on developing efficient and cost-effective energy storage technologies such as batteries, compressed air energy storage, or pumped hydro storage. These solutions will not only address intermittency issues but also provide a stable supply of electricity during peak demand periods.

3. Turbine Design and Efficiency:

Improving turbine efficiency and performance is crucial for maximizing energy production. Engineers should focus on developing advanced aerodynamic designs, materials, and control systems to increase turbine efficiency and reduce maintenance costs. Additionally, optimizing turbine placement and wind farm layouts can enhance overall energy production.

4. Environmental and Social Acceptance:

Wind farms often face opposition from local communities due to concerns about visual impact, noise, and wildlife impacts. Engineers should collaborate with stakeholders to address these concerns through innovative designs, improved noise-reducing technologies, and wildlife-friendly turbine designs. Public awareness campaigns can also help educate communities about the benefits of wind energy and dispel myths.

5. Transmission and Infrastructure:

Expanding wind energy production requires a well-developed transmission infrastructure to transport electricity from remote wind-rich areas to load centers. Engineers should work on improving transmission capacity, reducing transmission losses, and developing smart grid technologies that enable efficient electricity delivery.

Conclusion:

Overcoming the challenges in wind energy production is crucial for the United States to achieve energy independence and sustainability. By addressing grid integration, storage solutions, turbine design and efficiency, environmental concerns, and transmission infrastructure, engineers can pave the way for increased wind energy utilization. This subchapter highlights the importance of collaboration, innovation, and continuous research and development to overcome these challenges and unlock the full potential of wind energy in the United States.

Implementing wind farms and turbines

Wind energy has emerged as a crucial component in the United States' journey towards achieving energy independence. With its abundant resources and vast landscapes, the country has the potential to significantly increase wind energy production and utilization. This subchapter will explore the strategies and considerations involved in implementing wind farms and turbines, providing engineers with valuable insights into this rapidly growing sector.

To effectively implement wind farms, engineers must carefully assess various factors, including wind resource potential, land availability, and transmission infrastructure. Conducting comprehensive wind resource assessments is essential to identify suitable locations for wind farms. Engineers can utilize advanced modeling techniques and data analysis to determine the wind speed, direction, and variability in specific areas. This information enables them to select optimal sites for wind turbines, maximizing energy generation.

Once potential sites are identified, engineers must consider land availability and ownership rights. Collaborating with landowners, government agencies, and local communities is crucial to secure land leases and obtain necessary permits. Engineers should also assess the environmental impact of wind farms, ensuring compliance with regulations and minimizing any potential negative effects on wildlife, habitats, and aesthetics.

The successful implementation of wind farms also depends on robust transmission infrastructure. Engineers should evaluate existing power grids and identify potential upgrades or expansions to accommodate the increased capacity of wind energy. Collaborating with utility companies and regulatory bodies is essential to ensure seamless integration and reliable transmission of wind-generated electricity.

In terms of wind turbine technology, engineers play a vital role in selecting and designing efficient and reliable systems. They must consider factors such as turbine size, rotor diameter, tower height, and materials to optimize performance. Additionally, engineers should focus on improving turbine efficiency, reducing maintenance requirements, and enhancing grid compatibility.

To encourage the growth of wind energy, engineers can also contribute to research and development efforts. By exploring innovative designs, materials, and manufacturing processes, they can drive advancements in turbine technology, making wind energy more cost-effective and accessible.

In conclusion, implementing wind farms and turbines is a critical step towards achieving energy independence in the United States. Engineers have a crucial role to play in site selection, land acquisition, environmental assessments, transmission infrastructure, turbine technology, and research and development. By leveraging their expertise, engineers can contribute significantly to the expansion of wind energy production and utilization, helping the nation reduce its dependence on foreign oil imports and transition towards a self-sufficient future.

Integrating wind energy into the existing energy infrastructure

Integrating wind energy into the existing energy infrastructure is a crucial step towards achieving energy independence in the United States. As engineers, we have the responsibility to develop strategies that optimize the utilization of wind power to meet our growing energy demands. This subchapter will explore the challenges and opportunities associated with integrating wind energy into our existing infrastructure.

One of the key advantages of wind energy is its abundance and renewability. By harnessing the power of wind, we can reduce our dependence on fossil fuels and mitigate the harmful environmental impacts associated with traditional energy sources. However, integrating wind energy into the existing infrastructure is not without its challenges.

One of the major challenges is the intermittency of wind power. Unlike conventional power plants, wind turbines generate electricity only when the wind is blowing. This necessitates the development of effective energy storage solutions to bridge the gap between supply and demand.

Engineers play a critical role in developing advanced storage technologies, such as battery systems and pumped hydro storage, to ensure a stable and reliable power supply.

Another challenge is the transmission and distribution of wind energy. Wind farms are often located in remote areas with strong wind resources, which may be far away from population centers. This requires the expansion and upgrading of our transmission and distribution infrastructure to efficiently transport wind-generated electricity to where it is needed. Engineers can design and implement smart grid technologies that enable the seamless integration of wind power into the existing grid, ensuring optimal power flow and system stability.

Furthermore, engineers can contribute to the development of innovative wind turbine designs and technologies. Research and development efforts should focus on improving turbine efficiency, increasing power output, and reducing maintenance and operational costs. Advanced materials, such as carbon fiber composites, can be utilized to manufacture lighter and stronger turbine blades, enhancing overall performance and durability.

In conclusion, integrating wind energy into the existing energy infrastructure is essential for achieving energy independence in the United States. As engineers, we have the expertise to overcome the challenges associated with wind power integration. By developing advanced storage solutions, upgrading transmission and distribution infrastructure, and improving turbine technologies, we can maximize the utilization of wind energy and pave the way towards a self-sufficient future.

Investing in biofuel technologies

As engineers, we have a crucial role to play in finding sustainable and renewable energy solutions for the future. One area that holds great promise is biofuel technologies. In this subchapter, we will explore the importance of investing in biofuel technologies and their potential to contribute to the United States' goal of energy independence.

Biofuels are derived from renewable organic sources such as plants, algae, and agricultural waste. They offer several advantages over traditional fossil fuels, including lower greenhouse gas emissions, reduced dependence on foreign oil imports, and the potential for economic growth and job creation within the domestic market. By investing in biofuel technologies, we can take significant strides towards achieving energy independence in the United States.

One key area for investment is research and development. Engineers can contribute by developing more efficient and cost-effective biofuel production methods. This includes improving the conversion processes, optimizing feedstock selection, and enhancing the overall yield of biofuels. Research is also needed to explore new feedstock options, such as algae and non-food crops, which can offer higher energy yields and minimize competition with food production.

Another aspect to consider is the development of infrastructure to support biofuel production and distribution. This includes establishing biofuel refineries, storage facilities, and transportation networks. Engineers can play a vital role in designing and implementing the necessary infrastructure to ensure efficient and reliable biofuel production and distribution across the country.

Furthermore, collaboration between engineers, policymakers, and the private sector is essential to drive investment in biofuel technologies. This includes providing incentives for research and development, fostering public-private partnerships, and implementing policies that promote the use of biofuels in transportation, aviation, and other sectors. By working together, we can create a supportive environment for biofuel technologies to thrive and contribute to the nation's energy independence goals.

In conclusion, investing in biofuel technologies is a crucial step towards achieving energy independence in the United States. As engineers, we have the knowledge and skills to drive innovation and develop sustainable solutions for the future. By focusing on research and development, infrastructure development, and fostering collaboration, we can accelerate the adoption of biofuels and pave the way for a self-sufficient and sustainable energy future.

The potential of biofuels as a renewable energy source

Biofuels have emerged as a promising alternative to traditional fossil fuels, offering a renewable and sustainable solution to our energy needs. As engineers, it is imperative for us to explore the potential of biofuels in order to achieve energy independence in the United States. In this subchapter, we will delve into the various aspects of biofuels and their role in our quest for a self-sufficient future.

Biofuels, derived from organic matter such as plants and algae, offer several advantages over fossil fuels. Firstly, they are considered carbon-neutral, meaning they release an equal amount of carbon dioxide during combustion as they absorb during growth. This makes biofuels a cleaner and more environmentally friendly option. Additionally, biofuels can be produced domestically, reducing our dependence on foreign oil imports and improving national security.

One of the most promising biofuels is ethanol, which is primarily produced from corn in the United States. Ethanol can be blended with gasoline or used on its own as a transportation fuel. It offers a higher octane rating, lower emissions, and better engine performance compared to conventional gasoline. Furthermore, ethanol production stimulates the agricultural sector, creating jobs and boosting rural economies.

Another biofuel gaining traction is biodiesel, which is produced from vegetable oils or animal fats. Biodiesel can be used in diesel engines without any modifications and provides similar performance to petroleum-based diesel. It is biodegradable, non-toxic, and significantly reduces emissions of particulate matter and greenhouse gases.

To fully harness the potential of biofuels, it is crucial to invest in research and development. Engineers play a vital role in developing advanced technologies and processes that improve the efficiency and cost-effectiveness of biofuel production. This includes optimizing feedstock selection, developing new conversion methods, and enhancing the overall sustainability of biofuel supply chains.

In addition, policies and incentives should be implemented to promote the adoption of biofuels. This includes supporting the development of biofuel infrastructure, such as blending facilities and distribution networks. Government initiatives can also provide grants, tax credits, and loan guarantees to incentivize private investment in biofuel technologies.

By embracing biofuels as a renewable energy source, the United States can reduce its dependence on foreign oil, mitigate climate change, and stimulate economic growth. As engineers, we have the power to drive innovation and advance the biofuel industry, paving the way towards a self-sufficient future. Together, we can engineer a sustainable and resilient energy landscape for generations to come.

Challenges in biofuel production and distribution

Biofuels have emerged as a promising alternative to fossil fuels, offering the potential to reduce greenhouse gas emissions and decrease dependence on foreign oil imports. However, the production and distribution of biofuels come with their own set of challenges that need to be addressed to fully realize their potential.

One of the key challenges in biofuel production is the availability of feedstock. Biofuels can be derived from a variety of sources such as crops, agricultural residues, and algae. However, the production of biofuels on a large scale requires a significant amount of feedstock, which can put a strain on agricultural resources and lead to concerns over food security. Engineers need to find ways to optimize the use of feedstock and develop technologies to produce biofuels from non-food sources to overcome this challenge.

Another challenge is the conversion process from feedstock to biofuel. Different feedstocks require different conversion technologies, and each has its own set of technical and economic limitations. Engineers need to develop efficient and cost-effective conversion technologies that can handle a wide range of feedstocks and produce biofuels with high energy density and low emissions.

Once biofuels are produced, their distribution poses another challenge. The existing infrastructure for the distribution of fossil fuels is not always compatible with biofuels, which can have different physical and chemical properties. This requires engineers to design and retrofit distribution systems to accommodate biofuels, including storage tanks, pipelines, and fueling stations.

Furthermore, the cost of biofuel production is currently higher compared to fossil fuels, making it less economically viable. Engineers need to work on reducing production costs through technological advancements and economies of scale. Additionally, government incentives and policies can play a crucial role in making biofuels financially attractive for both producers and consumers.

Lastly, there is a need for robust quality control and certification systems to ensure the consistency and reliability of biofuels. Engineers must develop testing methods and standards to guarantee that biofuels meet the required specifications and can be used safely in existing engines and infrastructure.

In conclusion, while biofuels hold great promise in achieving energy independence and reducing environmental impact, several challenges need to be overcome. Engineers play a pivotal role in developing innovative technologies and solutions to address the challenges of biofuel production and distribution. By investing in research and development, implementing supportive policies, and collaborating with other stakeholders, engineers can help pave the way for a self-sufficient future powered by biofuels.

Strategies for promoting biofuel development

Biofuels have emerged as a promising alternative to traditional fossil fuels, offering a more sustainable and environmentally friendly option for meeting our energy needs. To ensure the United States becomes self-sufficient in energy, engineers must play a crucial role in developing and promoting biofuel technologies. This subchapter explores various strategies for advancing the development of biofuels and their integration into our energy infrastructure.

Investing in Research and Development:

One key strategy is to allocate significant resources to research and development in biofuel technologies. Engineers can lead the way in developing innovative and efficient processes for producing biofuels from organic materials such as agricultural residues, algae, and even waste products. By improving the efficiency of biofuel production, we can make it a more economically viable and scalable option for meeting our energy demands.

Collaborating with Agricultural Industry:

Another important strategy is to collaborate closely with the agricultural industry. Engineers can work with farmers to identify crops that are well-suited for biofuel production and develop efficient farming practices. By optimizing crop yields and reducing the input of fertilizers and pesticides, we can ensure that biofuel feedstocks are produced sustainably, without compromising food security or causing environmental harm.

Establishing Infrastructure:

Developing a robust infrastructure for biofuel production, distribution, and utilization is also crucial. Engineers can design and construct biofuel refineries and distribution networks, ensuring that biofuels can be easily integrated into the existing transportation system. Moreover, engineers can develop technologies for retrofitting existing vehicles and machinery to run on biofuels, making the transition to a biofuel-based economy more feasible.

Promoting Policy Support:

To accelerate the adoption of biofuels, engineers must advocate for policy support and incentives. This includes lobbying for government mandates that require a certain percentage of transportation fuel to come from renewable sources. Additionally, engineers can work with policymakers to establish tax credits and subsidies to encourage investment in biofuel technologies and infrastructure.

Educating the Public:

Finally, engineers must play a role in educating the public about the benefits of biofuels and dispelling any misconceptions. By raising awareness about the potential of biofuels to reduce greenhouse gas emissions, improve air quality, and enhance energy security, engineers can garner public support and drive demand for biofuels.

In conclusion, promoting biofuel development is a crucial strategy for achieving energy independence in the United States. Engineers can contribute significantly by investing in research and development, collaborating with the agricultural industry, establishing infrastructure, advocating for policy support, and educating the public. By harnessing the potential of biofuels, we can pave the way towards a more self-sufficient and sustainable energy future.

Incorporating biofuels into the transportation sector

As engineers, we play a crucial role in developing strategies for the United States to become self-sufficient in energy, including oil, and promoting the use of renewable energy sources. One viable solution to reduce our dependence on foreign oil imports and mitigate the environmental impact of fossil fuels is through the incorporation of biofuels into the transportation sector.

Biofuels, derived from organic matter such as crops, agricultural residues, and even algae, offer a promising alternative to traditional petroleum-based fuels. Not only do they have lower greenhouse gas emissions compared to fossil fuels, but they also provide an opportunity for domestic production, reducing our reliance on foreign oil.

To fully harness the potential of biofuels, we must invest in innovative technologies and infrastructure. Research and development in biofuel technologies should be encouraged to enhance production efficiency and explore new feedstock options. This includes developing advanced biofuels, such as cellulosic ethanol, which can be produced from non-food crops and waste materials.

Furthermore, promoting energy efficiency and conservation measures in the transportation sector can significantly reduce fuel consumption and increase the viability of biofuels. This can be achieved through the adoption of hybrid and electric vehicles, as well as the improvement of fuel efficiency standards for traditional vehicles.

In addition to technological advancements, policies must be implemented to support the adoption of biofuels. This includes providing incentives for the production and distribution of biofuels, such as tax credits and grants. Furthermore, fostering collaboration between government agencies, research institutions, and private industries can accelerate the development and deployment of biofuel technologies.

However, it is essential to ensure that biofuels are produced sustainably, without compromising food security or causing environmental harm. This requires implementing strict regulations and certification standards to prevent deforestation, land degradation, and water pollution associated with biofuel production.

By incorporating biofuels into the transportation sector, we can advance towards energy independence while reducing our carbon footprint. It is vital for engineers to actively contribute to the development of domestic biofuel infrastructure, collaborating with policymakers, researchers, and industry stakeholders to create a sustainable and resilient energy future for the United States. Together, we can drive the transition towards a self-sufficient and environmentally friendly transportation sector.

Promoting energy efficiency and conservation measures

In the pursuit of energy independence, it is crucial for engineers and policymakers to prioritize the promotion of energy efficiency and conservation measures. These strategies can significantly reduce the demand for energy, leading to a more sustainable and self-sufficient future for the United States.

Energy efficiency refers to the optimization of energy use in various sectors, including residential, commercial, and industrial. By implementing energy-efficient technologies and practices, engineers can ensure that energy is utilized in the most effective and economical way possible. This can be achieved through the use of energy-efficient appliances, advanced building insulation, and the adoption of smart grid systems.

Conservation measures, on the other hand, focus on reducing energy consumption by changing behavior and habits. This can be as simple as turning off lights when not in use, using natural lighting whenever possible, and practicing responsible heating and cooling practices. Engineers can contribute to conservation efforts by designing energy-efficient buildings and infrastructure that minimize energy waste.

To successfully promote energy efficiency and conservation measures, engineers need to collaborate with policymakers, businesses, and the general public. Educational campaigns can be launched to raise awareness about the benefits of energy efficiency and conservation, targeting both individuals and organizations. Engineers can lead by example by implementing these strategies in their own projects and advocating for their adoption in various sectors.

Additionally, financial incentives can be provided to encourage the implementation of energy-efficient technologies. Tax credits, grants, and subsidies can be offered to businesses and individuals who invest in energy-efficient equipment or retrofit their buildings to meet higher energy efficiency standards. This will not only drive the demand for energy-efficient technologies but also create job opportunities in the clean energy sector.

Furthermore, engineers can play a crucial role in conducting research and development activities to identify new technologies and practices that promote energy efficiency and conservation. This could involve developing more efficient renewable energy systems, improving energy storage technologies, and finding innovative ways to reduce energy consumption in various industries.

Overall, promoting energy efficiency and conservation measures is a key strategy for the United States to become self-sufficient in energy. By reducing energy demand and minimizing waste, engineers can help pave the way towards a more sustainable future, reducing the country's reliance on foreign energy sources and mitigating the environmental impacts of energy production and consumption.

Importance of energy efficiency and conservation

In today's world, energy efficiency and conservation have become critical components in our pursuit of a self-sufficient future. As engineers, it is our duty to understand the significance of these concepts and implement strategies that will help the United States achieve energy independence. This subchapter aims to shed light on the importance of energy efficiency and conservation, and how they can contribute to our overall goal.

Energy efficiency is the key to optimizing our energy consumption. By maximizing the output we get from each unit of energy input, we can minimize waste and reduce our reliance on external sources. This is particularly crucial when it comes to oil, which has been a major contributor to our energy needs. By employing efficient technologies and practices, such as advanced combustion engines and smart grid systems, we can improve fuel efficiency and reduce our dependence on oil imports.

Renewable energy strategies, such as solar power, wind energy, and biofuels, play a crucial role in our path to energy independence. However, without energy efficiency and conservation measures, their impact can be limited. By promoting energy-efficient appliances, buildings, and transportation systems, we can ensure that the energy generated from renewable sources is utilized optimally. This will not only reduce our carbon footprint but also enhance the overall sustainability of our energy systems.

Nuclear power is another clean energy source that can contribute significantly to our energy independence. However, it is essential to emphasize the importance of energy efficiency and conservation in this context as well. By implementing advanced reactor designs and efficient fuel cycles, we can maximize the utilization of nuclear energy while minimizing waste and environmental impact.

Furthermore, enhancing domestic natural gas production and distribution can provide us with a reliable and cleaner alternative to traditional fossil fuels. However, it is crucial to ensure that energy efficiency measures are in place to prevent wastage and promote responsible use of this valuable resource.

To achieve a self-sufficient future, it is imperative to invest in research and development of alternative energy sources. By encouraging innovation and technological advancements in areas such as hydrogen fuel cells, geothermal energy, and tidal power, we can diversify our energy portfolio and reduce our reliance on any single source.

In conclusion, energy efficiency and conservation are vital components in our journey towards energy independence. By implementing these measures, we can optimize our energy consumption, reduce waste, and lessen our dependence on foreign oil imports. To truly engineer a self-sufficient future, we must embrace energy-efficient technologies, promote sustainable practices, and invest in alternative energy sources. As engineers, we have the power to shape a more sustainable and self-reliant energy landscape for the United States.

Implementing energy-saving technologies and practices

Implementing energy-saving technologies and practices is crucial in the journey towards energy independence in the United States. Engineers play a pivotal role in developing and implementing these strategies to ensure a self-sufficient future. This subchapter will delve into various aspects of energy-saving technologies and practices that can be implemented across different sectors.

One key strategy to achieve energy independence is by promoting energy efficiency and conservation measures. This involves designing and implementing energy-efficient systems and practices in residential, commercial, and industrial buildings. Engineers can contribute by developing innovative technologies such as smart meters, energy-efficient lighting systems, and HVAC systems that optimize energy consumption.

Another important aspect is advancing nuclear power as a clean energy source. Engineers can work towards designing and building new nuclear power plants that are safer, more efficient, and produce less waste. Additionally, research and development efforts can focus on improving the efficiency of nuclear reactors and developing advanced nuclear technologies, such as small modular reactors.

Renewable energy strategies also play a vital role in achieving energy independence. Developing domestic solar power infrastructure is a key area where engineers can contribute. They can design and install solar panels, develop efficient energy storage systems, and optimize solar power generation. Similarly, engineers can work on increasing wind energy production and utilization by designing and implementing advanced wind turbines and optimizing wind farm layouts.

Investing in biofuel technologies is another important strategy. Engineers can research and develop advanced biofuel production techniques, such as cellulosic ethanol, algae-based biofuels, and biofuel production from agricultural waste. They can also contribute to the development of efficient biofuel conversion processes and infrastructure.

Furthermore, enhancing domestic natural gas production and distribution is crucial for energy independence. Engineers can employ advanced drilling techniques, such as hydraulic fracturing, to extract natural gas efficiently. They can also work on developing and implementing efficient natural gas distribution systems, including pipelines and storage facilities.

To reduce dependence on foreign oil imports, engineers can contribute by encouraging research and development in alternative energy sources. This includes exploring technologies such as geothermal energy, tidal energy, and hydrogen fuel cells. Engineers can also collaborate with policymakers to implement policies that incentivize the adoption of alternative energy sources and reduce reliance on foreign oil.

In conclusion, implementing energy-saving technologies and practices is essential for the United States to achieve energy independence. Engineers have a crucial role to play in developing and implementing strategies such as promoting energy efficiency, advancing nuclear power, developing renewable energy infrastructure, investing in biofuel technologies, and enhancing domestic natural gas production. By working together, engineers can pave the way towards a self-sufficient future for the United States.

Educating the public about energy conservation

In order to achieve true energy independence and sustainability in the United States, it is essential to not only implement innovative strategies and technologies but also to educate the public about the importance of energy conservation. As engineers, it is our responsibility to spread awareness and empower individuals to make energy-conscious choices in their daily lives.

One of the key ways to educate the public about energy conservation is through targeted awareness campaigns. By utilizing various platforms such as social media, television, and community events, we can reach a wider audience and emphasize the importance of reducing energy consumption. These campaigns can highlight the benefits of energy conservation, such as cost savings, environmental preservation, and the overall impact on national energy security.

Another effective approach is to collaborate with educational institutions and organizations to develop comprehensive energy conservation curricula. By integrating energy-saving practices into school programs, we can instill sustainable habits in the younger generation. This can be achieved through interactive workshops, energy audits, and hands-on projects that demonstrate the tangible impact of energy conservation.

Furthermore, it is crucial to engage communities and homeowners in energy conservation efforts. By organizing workshops and seminars, engineers can educate individuals on simple yet effective measures they can take to reduce their energy consumption. This can include tips on energy-efficient lighting, insulation, thermostat settings, and appliance usage. Additionally, engineers can provide guidance on available incentives and tax credits for energy-efficient upgrades, encouraging individuals to invest in sustainable technologies.

To maximize the impact of these efforts, it is important to involve local governments and policymakers. By advocating for policies that promote energy conservation, such as building codes that require energy-efficient designs and standards, we can create a supportive environment for sustainable practices. Additionally, engineers can collaborate with utility companies to offer energy efficiency programs, providing incentives for consumers to reduce their energy usage.

In conclusion, educating the public about energy conservation is a crucial aspect of achieving energy independence in the United States. As engineers, we have the knowledge and expertise to inform individuals about the benefits and practicality of energy conservation. By implementing targeted awareness campaigns, integrating energy conservation into educational curricula, engaging communities, and advocating for supportive policies, we can empower individuals to make informed choices and contribute to a self-sufficient future. Together, we can create a more sustainable and resilient energy landscape for the United States.

Government initiatives to encourage energy efficiency

Government initiatives play a crucial role in driving energy efficiency and promoting sustainable practices. In the United States, various programs and policies have been put in place to encourage energy efficiency in order to achieve a self-sufficient future. These initiatives aim to address the challenges of increasing energy demand, reducing greenhouse gas emissions, and minimizing reliance on foreign oil imports.

One of the key strategies to achieve energy independence is by developing renewable energy sources. The government has been actively investing in the development of domestic solar power infrastructure. By encouraging the installation of solar panels on rooftops and providing financial incentives, engineers can contribute to the growth of this sector. Similarly, increasing wind energy production and utilization is another focus area. The government offers tax credits and grants to support the expansion of wind farms and the development of wind turbine technologies.

Biofuel technologies are also being prioritized as a means to reduce dependence on fossil fuels. The government is investing in research and development to enhance the efficiency and sustainability of biofuel production. Engineers can contribute to this sector by designing and optimizing biofuel production processes.

Energy efficiency and conservation measures are critical in reducing energy consumption. The government has implemented policies to promote energy-efficient practices in buildings, transportation, and industries. This includes promoting the use of energy-efficient appliances, implementing building codes for energy-efficient construction, and encouraging the adoption of energy management systems in industries. Engineers can play a key role in designing energy-efficient systems and developing innovative technologies to conserve energy.

Advancing nuclear power as a clean energy source is another government initiative. Engineers can contribute to this sector by designing safer and more efficient nuclear reactors and improving waste management techniques.

In addition to renewable energy sources, the government is also focusing on expanding hydroelectric power generation and enhancing domestic natural gas production and distribution. These initiatives aim to utilize the country's existing resources and reduce reliance on foreign energy sources.

To foster innovation and explore alternative energy sources, the government encourages research and development in the energy sector. Grants and funding are provided to support research projects that aim to develop new technologies and improve the efficiency of existing ones.

Overall, the government sent initiatives discussed above are aimed at reducing energy consumption, diversifying the energy mix, and achieving energy independence. Engineers have a crucial role to play in implementing these strategies and developing sustainable solutions for a self-sufficient future.

Advancing nuclear power as a clean energy source

Nuclear power has long been recognized as a promising solution for meeting the ever-increasing energy demands of the United States. With its ability to generate massive amounts of electricity without emitting greenhouse gases, nuclear power can play a crucial role in our journey towards energy independence and a cleaner, more sustainable future. This subchapter explores the potential of advancing nuclear power as a clean energy source and the strategies that can be implemented to achieve this goal.

One of the key advantages of nuclear power is its reliability and capacity to provide baseload power. Unlike renewable energy sources like solar and wind, nuclear power plants can operate 24/7, ensuring a stable and constant supply of electricity. This makes nuclear power an ideal complement to intermittent renewable sources, helping to balance the grid and ensure a consistent power supply.

To advance nuclear power as a clean energy source, it is essential to invest in research and development to improve safety measures, increase efficiency, and reduce costs. This includes developing advanced reactor designs, such as small modular reactors (SMRs) and Generation IV reactors, which offer enhanced safety features, lower construction costs, and improved waste management.

Furthermore, streamlining the regulatory process and addressing public concerns about safety and waste disposal are crucial steps in promoting the expansion of nuclear power. By ensuring transparent and efficient licensing procedures, the implementation of new nuclear projects can be expedited, allowing for the timely deployment of advanced reactor technologies.

In addition to traditional nuclear power plants, the utilization of nuclear energy for other applications should also be explored. For instance, nuclear desalination plants can provide a sustainable solution to address the growing water scarcity issues in certain regions of the United States. By integrating nuclear power with desalination technologies, we can simultaneously generate clean electricity and produce freshwater, contributing to both energy independence and water security.

To maximize the benefits of nuclear power, collaboration between engineers, policymakers, and stakeholders is essential. By fostering partnerships, sharing best practices, and promoting knowledge exchange, we can accelerate the development and deployment of nuclear power as a clean energy source.

In conclusion, advancing nuclear power as a clean energy source holds immense potential for the United States' path towards energy independence and sustainability. Through investments in research and development, streamlined regulatory processes, and the exploration of innovative applications, nuclear power can play a significant role in reducing greenhouse gas emissions, ensuring a stable power supply, and driving economic growth. By embracing nuclear power as part of a diversified energy portfolio, we can pave the way for a self-sufficient future in which clean, reliable, and abundant energy is readily available for all.

Benefits and misconceptions of nuclear power

Nuclear power has long been a topic of both fascination and controversy. As engineers, it is crucial for us to understand the benefits and misconceptions surrounding this form of energy generation. In this subchapter, we will delve into the advantages of nuclear power and address common misconceptions that have hindered its widespread adoption.

One of the most significant benefits of nuclear power is its ability to produce vast amounts of electricity without emitting greenhouse gases.

As the United States strives for energy independence and reduces its reliance on foreign oil imports, nuclear power can play a crucial role in achieving this goal. By investing in nuclear power, we can decrease our carbon footprint and combat climate change, making it a viable option for reducing the country's overall emissions.

Another advantage of nuclear power is its reliability. Unlike renewable energy sources such as solar and wind, nuclear power plants can operate continuously, providing a stable source of electricity. This reliability is especially important as we seek to develop a self-sufficient energy infrastructure in the United States. By integrating nuclear power into our energy mix, we can ensure a consistent power supply, reducing the risk of blackouts and disruptions.

Furthermore, nuclear power has the potential to generate a significant amount of energy from a small amount of fuel. Compared to other energy sources, such as fossil fuels, nuclear power is incredibly efficient. This efficiency not only reduces the need for resource extraction but also minimizes waste production. Contrary to popular belief, the amount of nuclear waste generated is relatively small when compared to the amount of electricity produced. With advances in technology, we can continue to improve waste management and disposal methods, further enhancing the sustainability of nuclear power.

However, it is essential to address the misconceptions surrounding nuclear power. One of the most prevalent misconceptions is the safety concerns associated with nuclear accidents, such as the Chernobyl and Fukushima incidents. While these accidents were undoubtedly catastrophic, it is crucial to recognize that they were the result of outdated designs and inadequate safety measures. Modern nuclear power plants incorporate advanced safety features and protocols to prevent such accidents from occurring.

Another misconception is the association of nuclear power with nuclear weapons proliferation. While nuclear power does involve the use of radioactive materials, the risk of diversion for weapons purposes is highly regulated and monitored by international organizations such as the International Atomic Energy Agency (IAEA). The development and advancement of nuclear power can actually contribute to global security by reducing the demand for fossil fuels and potential conflicts over energy resources.

In conclusion, nuclear power offers numerous benefits for the United States in its pursuit of energy independence. By harnessing the power of nuclear energy, we can reduce greenhouse gas emissions, ensure a stable electricity supply, and utilize resources efficiently. However, it is crucial to dispel misconceptions surrounding nuclear power, such as safety concerns and weapons proliferation. Through proper regulations and advancements in technology, we can harness the full potential of nuclear power and engineer a self-sufficient future for the United States.

Overcoming challenges in nuclear power generation

Nuclear power has long been hailed as a clean and efficient energy source, capable of meeting the growing demands of a rapidly developing world. However, as with any complex technology, there are several challenges that need to be addressed in order to fully harness its potential. This subchapter will explore the various obstacles faced by nuclear power generation and discuss strategies to overcome them.

One of the primary challenges in nuclear power generation is the issue of waste disposal. Radioactive waste products have a long half-life and require specialized handling and storage facilities. Engineers have been working tirelessly to develop advanced waste management techniques, such as reprocessing and deep geological repositories, to ensure the safe and secure disposal of nuclear waste. These efforts must be intensified to address the concerns surrounding long-term waste storage.

Another significant challenge is the high upfront cost of nuclear power plants. The construction and maintenance of nuclear reactors require substantial financial investments. To overcome this obstacle, engineers can focus on optimizing the design and construction processes to reduce costs. Additionally, government incentives and funding can play a crucial role in making nuclear power more economically viable.

Safety concerns also pose a challenge to nuclear power generation. While accidents like the Chernobyl and Fukushima disasters are rare, they have had a lasting impact on public perception. Engineers must continue to enhance safety measures and develop innovative technologies to minimize the risk of accidents. This includes improved reactor designs, advanced monitoring systems, and robust emergency response plans.

Furthermore, public perception and acceptance of nuclear power remain a challenge. Misconceptions about radiation, nuclear accidents, and the disposal of radioactive waste often lead to opposition and resistance. It is essential for engineers to engage with the public, educate them about the benefits and safety of nuclear power, and address their concerns through transparent communication channels.

In conclusion, while nuclear power generation presents several challenges, engineers have the expertise and innovation to overcome them. By focusing on advanced waste management techniques, cost optimization, safety enhancements, and public engagement, nuclear power can be harnessed as a clean and efficient energy source. As the United States strives for energy independence and a reduced dependence on foreign oil imports, nuclear power must be considered as a vital component of a diverse and sustainable energy mix.

Strategies for expanding nuclear power capacity

In recent years, the need for energy independence has become increasingly pressing for the United States. As engineers, we play a crucial role in finding innovative solutions to meet this demand. One strategy that holds immense potential is the expansion of nuclear power capacity. Nuclear power has long been recognized as a clean and efficient source of energy, and by further developing this technology, we can significantly contribute to the goal of achieving energy self-sufficiency.

To expand nuclear power capacity, several key strategies can be implemented. First and foremost, it is essential to invest in the research and development of advanced nuclear technologies. This includes exploring new reactor designs that are safer, more efficient, and produce less waste. Additionally, efforts should be made to enhance the security and resilience of nuclear power plants to ensure their long-term viability.

Collaboration between the government and private sector is crucial for the successful expansion of nuclear power capacity. Public-private partnerships can help accelerate the deployment of new nuclear plants by providing financial incentives and streamlining regulatory processes. Moreover, government funding for research and development in nuclear energy should be increased to foster innovation and attract top talent to the field.

Another important strategy is to promote public awareness and acceptance of nuclear power. Educating the public about the safety and environmental benefits of nuclear energy is essential in dispelling misconceptions and overcoming resistance to its expansion. Engaging with local communities and addressing their concerns regarding waste disposal and plant safety can help build trust and gain public support.

Furthermore, international collaboration should be encouraged to leverage the expertise and resources of other countries. By sharing best practices and collaborating on research and development, we can accelerate the deployment of nuclear power and ensure its safe and efficient operation.

Expanding nuclear power capacity also requires a strong focus on workforce development. Investing in education and training programs for engineers and technicians specialized in nuclear energy will ensure a skilled workforce that can support the growth of the industry.

In conclusion, expanding nuclear power capacity is a critical strategy to achieve energy independence in the United States. By investing in research and development, fostering public acceptance, and promoting international collaboration, we can harness the full potential of nuclear energy and pave the way towards a self-sufficient future. As engineers, it is our responsibility to drive innovation and advocate for the expansion of nuclear power as a clean and efficient energy source.

Ensuring safety and waste management in nuclear energy

Nuclear energy has long been touted as a clean and efficient source of power that can help the United States achieve energy independence. However, it is crucial to address concerns regarding safety and waste management to ensure the successful implementation of nuclear power as a viable energy solution. Engineers play a pivotal role in developing strategies to maximize safety and minimize the environmental impact of nuclear energy.

One of the primary concerns associated with nuclear energy is the potential for accidents or meltdowns. Engineers have made significant advancements in reactor design and safety protocols to mitigate these risks. Modern nuclear power plants incorporate multiple layers of safety systems, such as redundant cooling systems and containment structures, to prevent the release of radioactive materials in the event of an accident. Additionally, ongoing research and development efforts are focused on developing even safer reactor designs, including advanced passive cooling systems that do not rely on external power sources.

Another crucial aspect of ensuring the safety of nuclear energy is effective waste management. Nuclear power generates radioactive waste that must be handled and stored appropriately to prevent environmental contamination. Engineers are working on developing advanced waste treatment technologies, such as vitrification and transmutation, to reduce the volume and radioactivity of nuclear waste. Additionally, secure long-term storage solutions, such as deep geological repositories, are being explored to ensure the safe disposal of radioactive materials.

To further enhance safety and waste management in nuclear energy, engineers are also actively involved in improving operational practices and regulatory frameworks. Continuous training and education programs are implemented to ensure that personnel operating nuclear plants are well-equipped to handle any potential emergencies. Additionally, strict regulations are enforced to monitor and enforce safety standards in the nuclear industry.

In conclusion, engineers play a vital role in ensuring the safety and waste management of nuclear energy. Through continuous research and development efforts, they are working on enhancing reactor designs, developing advanced waste treatment technologies, and improving operational practices. By addressing safety concerns and implementing effective waste management strategies, nuclear energy can be harnessed as a clean and reliable energy source, contributing to the United States' goal of achieving energy independence.

Expanding hydroelectric power generation

Hydroelectric power has long been recognized as a reliable and sustainable source of energy. In recent years, there has been a growing emphasis on expanding hydroelectric power generation in the United States as part of a broader strategy to achieve energy independence. This subchapter explores the various ways in which engineers can contribute to the expansion of hydroelectric power generation and its integration into the national energy grid.

One of the key aspects of expanding hydroelectric power generation is the construction of new hydroelectric dams. Engineers play a crucial role in designing and constructing these large-scale infrastructure projects. They must consider factors such as the availability of suitable sites, environmental impact assessments, and the technical feasibility of the project. By employing innovative engineering techniques, engineers can optimize the design of dams to maximize power generation while minimizing their environmental footprint.

In addition to building new dams, engineers can also contribute to the enhancement of existing hydroelectric facilities. This can involve retrofitting older dams with more efficient turbines and generators, as well as implementing advanced control systems to optimize power output. Engineers can also explore the potential for small-scale hydroelectric installations in rivers and streams that were previously considered unsuitable for traditional dam construction. These smaller projects can provide localized power generation and contribute to the overall diversification of the energy mix.

Integration of hydroelectric power into the national energy grid is another important consideration. Engineers can develop smart grid technologies that enable the efficient transmission and distribution of hydroelectric power. This includes the development of advanced monitoring and control systems that optimize the utilization of hydroelectric resources and ensure a stable and reliable power supply.

It is worth noting that the expansion of hydroelectric power generation should be pursued in a manner that is environmentally sustainable. Engineers must work closely with environmental scientists and policymakers to ensure that new projects are designed and operated in a manner that minimizes their impact on ecosystems and local communities. This may involve the implementation of fish passage systems to mitigate the effects of dams on aquatic life, as well as the adoption of best practices for sediment management and water quality protection.

In conclusion, expanding hydroelectric power generation is a key strategy for achieving energy independence in the United States. Engineers have a critical role to play in designing and constructing new hydroelectric dams, enhancing existing facilities, and integrating hydroelectric power into the national energy grid. By leveraging their technical expertise and collaborating with other stakeholders, engineers can contribute to the development of a self-sufficient and sustainable energy future for the United States.

Harnessing the power of water for electricity

Hydroelectric power generation has long been recognized as a reliable and sustainable source of electricity. In this subchapter, we will explore the potential of harnessing the power of water to contribute to the United States' goal of energy independence.

Hydroelectric power plants convert the energy of flowing water into electricity by using turbines and generators. These plants can be built on rivers, dams, or even ocean tides, making them versatile and adaptable to various geographical locations. One of the major advantages of hydroelectric power is its ability to provide a consistent and reliable source of electricity, as water flow can be controlled and regulated.

The United States has enormous untapped potential for hydroelectric power generation. With an abundance of rivers and water resources, the country has the opportunity to significantly increase its hydroelectric capacity. Expanding hydroelectric power generation not only contributes to energy independence but also helps reduce greenhouse gas emissions, as hydroelectric plants produce minimal carbon dioxide.

To fully harness the power of water for electricity, engineers must focus on two key aspects: increasing the number of hydroelectric power plants and improving the efficiency of existing ones. By constructing new plants in suitable locations and retrofitting older facilities with modern technology, we can maximize the power output and minimize environmental impacts.

Furthermore, advancements in turbine technology can greatly enhance the efficiency of hydroelectric power generation. Engineers can explore innovative designs and materials to improve turbine performance, leading to higher conversion rates and increased electricity output. Additionally, the development of fish-friendly turbines can mitigate the impact on aquatic ecosystems, ensuring a sustainable balance between energy production and environmental conservation.

However, it is important to consider the potential challenges associated with expanding hydroelectric power generation. Environmental concerns, such as the alteration of river ecosystems and the displacement of wildlife, must be carefully addressed. Engineers should collaborate with environmental scientists and policymakers to develop strategies that minimize the negative impacts on biodiversity and maintain the ecological integrity of water bodies.

In conclusion, expanding hydroelectric power generation is a crucial step towards achieving energy independence in the United States. By harnessing the power of water, we can secure a reliable and sustainable source of electricity while reducing our dependence on foreign oil imports. Engineers have a pivotal role to play in developing and implementing strategies that maximize the potential of hydroelectric power generation while mitigating its environmental impacts. Through innovation and collaboration, we can pave the way for a self-sufficient future powered by clean and renewable energy.

Challenges in hydroelectric power production

Hydroelectric power production is a crucial component of the strategies for the United States to become self-sufficient in energy. As engineers, it is important to be aware of the challenges that exist in this field to ensure the effective development and utilization of this renewable energy source.

One of the primary challenges in hydroelectric power production is the availability of suitable sites for hydropower plants. The construction of dams and reservoirs requires specific geological conditions and a sufficient supply of water. Identifying and assessing these sites can be a complex and time-consuming process, requiring extensive research and analysis.

Another challenge is the environmental impact of hydropower facilities. While hydroelectric power is considered a clean and renewable energy source, the construction of dams can have significant effects on the surrounding ecosystems. It can disrupt natural river flows, alter water quality, and affect aquatic habitats. Engineers must carefully consider these environmental impacts and work towards minimizing them through innovative design and mitigation measures.

Maintaining and managing hydropower infrastructure is yet another challenge in hydroelectric power production. Dams, turbines, and other components of hydropower plants require regular maintenance and repairs to ensure their efficient operation. Engineers need to develop strategies for monitoring and addressing the aging infrastructure to prevent potential failures and ensure the long-term reliability and safety of these facilities.

Furthermore, hydroelectric power production is dependent on climatic conditions and water availability. Droughts, seasonal variations, and changing precipitation patterns can significantly impact the generation capacity of hydropower plants. Engineers must develop strategies to manage and mitigate these risks, such as implementing advanced forecasting models and exploring alternative water sources.

Lastly, there are regulatory and policy challenges that need to be addressed. The development of hydropower projects often involves complex permitting processes, environmental assessments, and compliance with various regulations. Engineers need to navigate through these legal and regulatory frameworks effectively to ensure the successful implementation of hydroelectric power projects.

Despite these challenges, hydroelectric power production remains a viable and important component of the United States' energy independence strategy. Through innovative engineering solutions, careful environmental planning, and effective policy frameworks, engineers can overcome these challenges and contribute to the expansion of hydroelectric power generation in the country.

Strategies for increasing hydroelectric capacity

Introduction:

Hydroelectric power is a reliable and renewable source of energy that plays a crucial role in the United States' pursuit of energy independence. To further harness the potential of this clean energy source, engineers must focus on implementing strategies to increase hydroelectric capacity. This subchapter will explore various approaches to expanding hydroelectric power generation, ensuring a sustainable and self-sufficient future for the United States.

1. Upgrading Existing Infrastructure:

One strategy involves upgrading and modernizing existing hydroelectric power plants. By optimizing turbines, generators, and transmission systems, engineers can significantly increase the efficiency and output of these facilities. Additionally, adopting advanced control systems can enhance grid integration and improve overall performance.

2. Constructing New Hydroelectric Facilities:

Building new hydroelectric dams and power plants in suitable locations can significantly augment the capacity of hydroelectric power generation. Engineers should identify potential sites with favorable topography, water flow, and proximity to transmission networks. Utilizing advanced construction techniques and incorporating environmental considerations will be crucial in this process.

3. Incorporating Pumped Storage:

Pumped storage hydroelectricity is a promising technology that can address the intermittent nature of renewable energy sources. Engineers must focus on designing and constructing pumped storage facilities, which store excess electricity during periods of low demand and release it during peak consumption. This approach not only enhances hydroelectric capacity but also helps stabilize the grid.

4. Encouraging Small-Scale Hydroelectric Projects:

Developing small-scale hydroelectric projects can be an effective strategy to increase capacity while minimizing environmental impacts. Engineers should explore opportunities to harness energy from water streams, rivers, and irrigation systems. Implementing micro-hydro turbines and run-of-river systems can provide localized power generation and reduce reliance on centralized facilities.

5. Improving Environmental Mitigation Measures:

To ensure sustainable hydroelectric development, engineers must prioritize environmental mitigation measures. Implementing fish passage systems, habitat restoration initiatives, and sediment management strategies can help mitigate the ecological impacts associated with dams and hydroelectric projects.

Conclusion:

Expanding hydroelectric power generation is vital for achieving energy independence in the United States. By upgrading existing infrastructure, constructing new facilities, incorporating pumped storage, encouraging small-scale projects, and implementing environmental mitigation measures, engineers can significantly increase hydroelectric capacity. These strategies, combined with other renewable energy sources, will pave the way for a self-sufficient future, reduce dependence on foreign oil imports, and contribute to a cleaner and more sustainable energy landscape.

Balancing environmental concerns with hydropower development

Hydropower is a vital component of the United States' strategy for energy independence. It is a clean, renewable source that can provide a significant portion of the country's power needs. However, the development of hydropower must be balanced with environmental concerns to ensure the long-term sustainability of this energy source.

One of the primary environmental concerns associated with hydropower development is the impact on aquatic ecosystems. Dams can disrupt the natural flow of rivers, leading to changes in water temperature, sedimentation, and the migration patterns of fish. To address these concerns, engineers must design and implement mitigation measures such as fish ladders, bypass channels, and improved downstream fish passage systems. These measures can help maintain the ecological balance of rivers and protect vulnerable species.

Another environmental consideration is the alteration of downstream water quality. The accumulation of sediment, changes in dissolved oxygen levels, and the release of pollutants from reservoirs can have adverse effects on aquatic life. Engineers can minimize these impacts by designing effective sedimentation management systems, implementing water quality monitoring programs, and utilizing innovative technologies to treat and manage wastewater.

In addition to the direct environmental impacts, hydropower development can also have indirect effects on terrestrial ecosystems. The creation of reservoirs can result in the flooding of large areas, leading to habitat loss and the displacement of wildlife. To mitigate these impacts, engineers can work closely with ecologists and conservationists to identify and protect critical habitats, implement reforestation and habitat restoration programs, and establish wildlife corridors to facilitate the movement of species.

Furthermore, the construction of hydropower plants often requires the clearing of land and the diversion of rivers. This can result in the loss of valuable ecosystems, including wetlands and riparian zones. To minimize these impacts, engineers can adopt sustainable construction practices, such as utilizing low-impact development techniques, implementing erosion and sediment control measures, and restoring impacted areas after construction is completed.

Balancing environmental concerns with hydropower development requires a multidisciplinary approach that involves collaboration between engineers, scientists, policymakers, and local communities. By integrating environmental considerations into the planning, design, and operation of hydropower projects, engineers can ensure that the benefits of this clean energy source are maximized while minimizing its impact on the environment. This approach will contribute to the United States' goal of becoming self-sufficient in energy and reducing its dependence on foreign oil imports, while also safeguarding the natural resources upon which our ecosystems and communities depend.

Enhancing domestic natural gas production and distribution

To achieve energy independence and promote a self-sufficient future for the United States, it is crucial to focus on enhancing domestic natural gas production and distribution. Natural gas is a clean and abundant source of energy that can play a significant role in reducing our dependence on foreign oil imports, lowering greenhouse gas emissions, and creating job opportunities for engineers across the country.

One strategy to enhance domestic natural gas production is through the exploration and development of shale gas resources. Shale gas has revolutionized the energy industry in recent years, and engineers have played a vital role in developing innovative techniques such as hydraulic fracturing and horizontal drilling. Continued investments in research and development will enable engineers to improve these techniques, making shale gas extraction more efficient and environmentally friendly.

Furthermore, the construction of new natural gas infrastructure is essential to ensure the efficient distribution of this valuable resource. Engineers can contribute to the development of pipelines, storage facilities, and liquefied natural gas (LNG) terminals, enabling the transportation and storage of natural gas across the country. These infrastructure projects will not only create jobs but also enhance the reliability and flexibility of the natural gas supply.

In addition to conventional natural gas, engineers can explore the potential of renewable natural gas (RNG). RNG is produced from organic waste sources such as landfills, wastewater treatment plants, and agricultural waste. By utilizing innovative technologies, engineers can capture and convert these waste gases into a valuable energy source. This process not only reduces greenhouse gas emissions but also provides a sustainable and renewable alternative to traditional natural gas.

To encourage domestic natural gas production and distribution, it is crucial to create favorable policies and regulatory frameworks. These policies should focus on streamlining the permitting process, incentivizing investment in natural gas infrastructure, and promoting research and development in advanced natural gas technologies. Moreover, collaboration between government agencies, industry stakeholders, and engineers is vital to ensure effective coordination and implementation of these strategies.

By enhancing domestic natural gas production and distribution, the United States can reduce its dependence on foreign oil imports, promote cleaner energy sources, and create a more resilient and self-sufficient energy future. Engineers play a critical role in developing and implementing these strategies, utilizing their expertise to improve extraction techniques, construct infrastructure, and explore innovative technologies. Through their efforts, engineers can contribute to a more sustainable and prosperous energy landscape for the United States.

Importance of natural gas as a transitional energy source

As engineers, it is crucial for us to understand the significance of natural gas as a transitional energy source in our journey towards achieving energy independence in the United States. Natural gas plays a pivotal role in several strategies aimed at reducing our dependence on foreign oil imports and promoting the development and utilization of renewable energy sources.

One of the primary reasons natural gas holds such importance is its abundance in domestic reserves. The United States has vast natural gas reserves, making it a valuable asset in our pursuit of energy self-sufficiency. By enhancing domestic natural gas production and distribution, we can reduce our reliance on foreign sources, ensuring a more secure and stable energy supply.

Additionally, natural gas serves as an excellent complement to renewable energy sources such as solar and wind power. While renewables have the potential to provide clean, sustainable energy, they are intermittent in nature. Natural gas provides a reliable and flexible energy source that can fill in the gaps when renewable energy generation is insufficient. This ensures a consistent and uninterrupted power supply, even during periods of low sunlight or wind.

Furthermore, natural gas is a cleaner-burning fossil fuel compared to coal and oil. It produces significantly lower levels of carbon dioxide and other harmful emissions, making it a more environmentally friendly choice. As we strive to reduce greenhouse gas emissions and combat climate change, transitioning from coal and oil to natural gas can play a crucial role in achieving our sustainability goals.

In terms of energy efficiency, natural gas also offers several advantages. It can be used for combined heat and power (CHP) systems, where the waste heat generated during electricity production is captured and utilized for heating or cooling purposes. This improves overall energy efficiency and reduces energy wastage, making natural gas an attractive option for engineers focused on promoting energy conservation measures.

Lastly, natural gas serves as a bridge to future energy technologies. While we continue to invest in research and development of alternative energy sources, such as hydrogen or advanced battery technologies, natural gas provides a reliable and readily available energy source. It allows us to transition gradually towards a more sustainable energy future without sacrificing the stability and reliability of our energy infrastructure.

In conclusion, natural gas holds immense importance as a transitional energy source in our quest for energy independence. Its abundance, versatility, environmental benefits, energy efficiency, and role as a complement to renewable energy sources make it a vital component of the strategies outlined in this book. By enhancing domestic natural gas production and distribution, we can reduce dependence on foreign oil imports, bolster renewable energy development, and pave the way towards a self-sufficient and sustainable energy future in the United States.

Challenges in natural gas extraction and distribution

Natural gas has long been recognized as a crucial component in the quest for energy independence in the United States. It is a cleaner-burning fuel compared to coal and oil, making it an attractive option for reducing greenhouse gas emissions and addressing climate change concerns. However, the extraction and distribution of natural gas come with their own set of challenges that need to be addressed for a self-sufficient future.

One of the primary challenges in natural gas extraction is the process of hydraulic fracturing, commonly known as fracking. Fracking involves injecting large volumes of water, sand, and chemicals into underground rock formations to release trapped natural gas. However, this technique has faced criticism due to potential environmental impacts, such as groundwater contamination and seismic activity. Engineers play a crucial role in developing and implementing technologies that minimize these risks and ensure responsible extraction practices.

Another challenge lies in the transportation and distribution of natural gas. While pipelines are the most common method for transporting natural gas, they face various hurdles. Constructing pipelines requires extensive planning, land acquisition, and environmental considerations. Moreover, aging pipeline infrastructure poses safety concerns and requires regular maintenance and upgrades. Engineers need to develop innovative solutions for pipeline construction, monitoring, and maintenance to ensure safe and efficient distribution of natural gas across the country.

Additionally, the expansion of natural gas production comes with the challenge of balancing supply and demand. As the United States aims for energy independence, it needs to develop a robust storage and distribution system to manage fluctuations in demand and supply. This requires strategic planning and investment in storage facilities, such as underground storage reservoirs and liquefied natural gas terminals. Engineers can contribute by designing and optimizing these systems to ensure reliable and efficient delivery of natural gas to consumers.

In conclusion, while natural gas offers significant benefits in the pursuit of energy independence, it is not without its challenges. Engineers play a vital role in addressing these challenges through the development of responsible extraction techniques, efficient transportation methods, and storage and distribution systems. By overcoming these obstacles, the United States can enhance its domestic natural gas production and distribution, reducing its dependence on foreign energy sources and moving closer to achieving self-sufficiency in energy.

Strategies for increasing domestic natural gas production

As engineers, it is crucial for us to explore and implement strategies that can help the United States become self-sufficient in energy. One such strategy is to focus on increasing domestic natural gas production. Natural gas is a cleaner alternative to traditional fossil fuels, and its abundance in the United States makes it a viable option for achieving energy independence.

To enhance domestic natural gas production, we need to adopt a multi-faceted approach. Firstly, investing in advanced drilling technologies such as hydraulic fracturing and horizontal drilling can help access previously untapped reserves. These techniques allow us to extract natural gas from shale formations, significantly expanding our domestic production capacity.

Additionally, promoting research and development in the field of natural gas exploration and production can lead to innovative solutions. This includes developing new drilling techniques that are more efficient and environmentally friendly, as well as improving the extraction process to minimize waste and emissions.

Furthermore, it is essential to invest in the infrastructure necessary for transporting and distributing natural gas. This includes expanding and upgrading pipelines, storage facilities, and liquefied natural gas (LNG) terminals. By improving the infrastructure, we can ensure that the natural gas produced domestically can be efficiently transported and utilized across the country.

Incentivizing the use of natural gas in various sectors is another strategy to increase domestic production. This can be achieved by offering tax incentives or subsidies to industries that switch to natural gas as their primary energy source. Additionally, promoting the use of natural gas in transportation, such as through the development of natural gas-powered vehicles or supporting the construction of refueling stations, can further stimulate demand and production.

Lastly, it is crucial to prioritize environmental considerations and ensure responsible production practices. This includes implementing strict regulations on drilling operations to protect groundwater resources and prevent the release of harmful pollutants. By adopting sustainable practices, we can strike a balance between increasing domestic natural gas production and preserving the environment.

In conclusion, increasing domestic natural gas production is a vital strategy for achieving energy independence in the United States. By investing in advanced drilling technologies, promoting research and development, improving infrastructure, incentivizing usage, and implementing responsible production practices, we can maximize our natural gas reserves and reduce dependence on foreign energy sources. As engineers, it is our responsibility to drive these strategies forward and contribute to a self-sufficient future.

Expanding natural gas infrastructure and utilization

In this subchapter, we will explore the importance of expanding natural gas infrastructure and utilization as a crucial step towards achieving energy independence in the United States. As engineers, it is our responsibility to develop innovative strategies that can optimize the utilization of natural gas resources and promote its widespread adoption.

Natural gas is a versatile and abundant source of energy that offers several advantages over other fossil fuels. It is cleaner, emitting fewer greenhouse gases and pollutants compared to coal and oil. Furthermore, it is more efficient and affordable, making it an attractive option for both industrial and residential use.

To fully harness the potential of natural gas, it is imperative to invest in the expansion of infrastructure. This includes the construction of pipelines, storage facilities, and liquefaction plants. By enhancing the distribution network, we can ensure a reliable supply of natural gas to meet the growing demand across the country.

To encourage the utilization of natural gas, we must also focus on developing technologies that can optimize its efficiency. This includes the advancement of combined heat and power systems, which generate both electricity and useful heat from natural gas. By capturing and utilizing waste heat, we can significantly increase overall energy efficiency and reduce greenhouse gas emissions.

Furthermore, we should promote the adoption of natural gas vehicles (NGVs) as an alternative to traditional gasoline and diesel vehicles. NGVs offer lower fuel costs, reduced emissions, and improved energy security. To support this transition, we need to establish a robust network of refueling stations and incentivize the production and purchase of NGVs.

In addition to infrastructure development, research and development efforts should focus on improving the extraction techniques of natural gas, such as hydraulic fracturing, to minimize environmental impacts. We must also invest in the development of renewable natural gas (RNG) sources, such as biogas from organic waste, to further reduce the carbon footprint associated with natural gas utilization.

Expanding natural gas infrastructure and utilization is a crucial step towards achieving energy independence. By leveraging this abundant and cleaner energy source, we can reduce our dependence on foreign oil imports and contribute to a more sustainable future. As engineers, we have the expertise and ingenuity to drive this transformation and lead the United States towards self-sufficiency in energy.

Encouraging research and development in alternative energy sources

The pursuit of energy independence has become an urgent priority for the United States. To achieve this goal, engineers play a pivotal role in developing innovative strategies and technologies that harness alternative energy sources. This subchapter explores the importance of encouraging research and development in alternative energy sources and highlights the potential benefits it holds for the nation's energy future.

Alternative energy sources offer a promising solution to mitigate the environmental impact of traditional energy production methods while reducing dependence on foreign oil imports. Engineers can spearhead research and development efforts in this field by focusing on a wide range of technologies, including solar power, wind energy, biofuels, nuclear power, hydroelectric power, and natural gas. By investing in these areas, the United States can pave the way for a self-sufficient energy future.

Research and development in alternative energy sources present numerous advantages. Firstly, it allows engineers to enhance the efficiency and affordability of renewable energy technologies. Through continuous innovation, engineers can refine existing technologies, develop new materials, and optimize system designs to maximize energy production. This will contribute to the expansion of renewable energy sources and make them more accessible to a wider range of consumers.

Moreover, research and development in alternative energy can lead to job creation and economic growth. As the United States increasingly relies on renewable energy sources, there will be a surge in demand for skilled engineers, technicians, and manufacturing workers. This will create employment opportunities in various sectors and stimulate economic development in regions that embrace renewable energy.

Furthermore, encouraging research and development in alternative energy sources can strengthen the nation's energy security. By diversifying the energy mix, the United States becomes less vulnerable to geopolitical tensions and market fluctuations associated with traditional energy sources. Alternative energy technologies can be developed domestically, reducing dependence on foreign energy imports and enhancing national resilience.

To encourage research and development in alternative energy sources, it is crucial to provide financial incentives and support for engineers and researchers. Government funding programs, tax incentives, and grants can stimulate innovation and attract talent to the field. Collaboration between academia, industry, and government agencies is also vital to foster knowledge sharing and accelerate progress in alternative energy research.

In conclusion, encouraging research and development in alternative energy sources is crucial for the United States to achieve energy independence. Engineers play a vital role in driving innovation and developing technologies that harness the power of renewable energy. By investing in research and development, the nation can enhance the efficiency, affordability, and accessibility of alternative energy sources while creating jobs, bolstering economic growth, and reducing dependence on foreign oil imports.

Importance of innovation in energy technology

The Importance of Innovation in Energy Technology

Innovation in energy technology is crucial for the United States to achieve self-sufficiency in energy and reduce its dependence on foreign imports. Engineers play a pivotal role in driving this innovation, as they possess the expertise and knowledge required to develop groundbreaking solutions. This subchapter explores the significance of innovation in various energy sectors and highlights the strategies that engineers can employ to propel the United States towards energy independence.

One of the key strategies for achieving energy independence is by developing renewable energy sources. Engineers can contribute to this goal by designing and implementing advanced technologies to harness solar power. By investing in domestic solar power infrastructure, the United States can tap into its abundant solar resources and significantly reduce reliance on traditional energy sources. Similarly, engineers can focus on increasing wind energy production and utilization, as wind power has immense potential to provide clean and sustainable energy.

Biofuels also hold promise as an alternative energy source, and engineers can play a vital role in advancing biofuel technologies. By investing in research and development, engineers can develop more efficient and cost-effective methods for producing biofuels, ultimately reducing the nation's dependence on fossil fuels.

Furthermore, promoting energy efficiency and conservation measures is essential for achieving self-sufficiency. Engineers can design energy-efficient buildings, appliances, and transportation systems, ensuring that energy consumption is minimized without compromising functionality and comfort. Additionally, engineers can advance nuclear power as a clean energy source by developing safer and more efficient reactor designs.

Hydroelectric power generation is another area where engineers can make significant contributions. By expanding the use of hydroelectric power, engineers can harness the immense energy potential of water resources, providing a reliable and sustainable source of electricity.

In addition to renewable energy sources, engineers can enhance domestic natural gas production and distribution. By optimizing extraction techniques and improving infrastructure, engineers can ensure a stable supply of natural gas, reducing reliance on imports.

To foster innovation in energy technology, it is crucial to encourage research and development in alternative energy sources. By providing funding and support to engineers and scientists, the United States can accelerate the development of cutting-edge technologies that will revolutionize the energy sector.

Lastly, implementing policies to reduce dependence on foreign oil imports is vital. By incentivizing the use of alternative energy sources and supporting domestic production, engineers can contribute to reducing the nation's reliance on oil and promoting energy independence.

In conclusion, innovation in energy technology is of paramount importance for the United States to achieve self-sufficiency in energy. Engineers have a crucial role to play in developing strategies for renewable energy, advancing nuclear power, enhancing natural gas production, and promoting energy efficiency. By embracing innovation and investing in research and development, engineers can drive the nation towards a self-sufficient future, reducing dependence on foreign imports and ensuring a sustainable and secure energy supply for generations to come.

Funding and supporting research in alternative energy

In order to engineer a self-sufficient future and achieve energy independence, it is crucial to invest in and support research in alternative energy sources. Through funding and strategic support, engineers can drive the development of innovative technologies and solutions that will revolutionize the energy landscape in the United States. This subchapter explores various strategies for funding and supporting research in alternative energy, focusing on the niches of strategies for the United States to become self-sufficient in energy, including oil, and renewable energy strategies for the United States.

One of the key steps towards energy independence is developing domestic solar power infrastructure. Engineers should actively seek funding opportunities to advance solar energy research and development, aiming to optimize efficiency and reduce costs. By leveraging federal grants and private investments, engineers can pioneer breakthroughs in solar panel technology, storage systems, and grid integration, ultimately expanding the deployment of solar power across the nation.

Another promising avenue is increasing wind energy production and utilization. Engineers should advocate for increased funding for wind energy research, with a focus on improving turbine design, increasing efficiency, and mitigating environmental impacts. By collaborating with researchers, government agencies, and industry stakeholders, engineers can drive advancements in wind energy technology and contribute to the expansion of wind farms in suitable regions across the United States.

Investing in biofuel technologies is another vital aspect of achieving energy independence. Engineers should actively engage in research and development efforts to enhance the efficiency and sustainability of biofuel production processes. This includes exploring advanced feedstock options, optimizing conversion technologies, and developing new methods for biofuel distribution and utilization. Through strategic partnerships and government funding, engineers can accelerate the commercialization of biofuels and reduce the nation's reliance on fossil fuels.

Furthermore, promoting energy efficiency and conservation measures is critical to reducing energy consumption and achieving self-sufficiency. Engineers should collaborate with policymakers and industry leaders to develop and implement energy-efficient technologies and practices. By investing in research and development, engineers can advance energy-efficient building materials, smart grid systems, and energy management technologies, leading to significant energy savings across various sectors.

In conclusion, funding and supporting research in alternative energy is paramount for engineers to engineer a self-sufficient future. By focusing on strategies such as developing domestic solar power infrastructure, increasing wind energy production, investing in biofuel technologies, promoting energy efficiency, and advancing nuclear power, engineers can contribute to the United States' path towards energy independence. Through collaboration, innovation, and strategic funding, engineers can pave the way for a sustainable and prosperous future for the nation while reducing dependence on foreign oil imports.

Collaboration between academia and industry

Collaboration between academia and industry is crucial in the pursuit of strategies for the United States to become self-sufficient in energy. As engineers, we have the responsibility to bridge the gap between theoretical knowledge and practical application, and this collaboration allows us to do just that. By working together, academia and industry can combine their expertise, resources, and innovative ideas to accelerate the development and implementation of sustainable energy solutions.

One area where this collaboration is particularly important is in the development of domestic solar power infrastructure. Academia can contribute by conducting research to improve the efficiency and affordability of solar panels, while industry can bring these innovations to the market and scale up production. Together, they can also work on integrating solar power into the existing energy grid and developing storage technologies to address the intermittent nature of solar energy.

Similarly, academia and industry can collaborate to increase wind energy production and utilization. Academic institutions can conduct studies to identify the most suitable locations for wind farms and develop advanced turbine designs. Industry can then use this knowledge to build and operate wind farms, harnessing the power of the wind to generate clean electricity.

Investing in biofuel technologies is another area where collaboration is vital. Academia can focus on researching and developing new biofuel production methods, such as algae-based or cellulosic biofuels, while industry can invest in large-scale production facilities and distribution networks. By working together, they can overcome technical and economic challenges, making biofuels a viable alternative to fossil fuels.

Furthermore, collaboration between academia and industry is essential for advancing nuclear power as a clean energy source. Academia can contribute by conducting research on advanced reactor designs and safety measures, while industry can apply this knowledge to build and operate nuclear power plants. Together, they can work towards optimizing the efficiency and safety of nuclear power, addressing concerns about waste disposal and non-proliferation.

In addition to these specific areas, collaboration between academia and industry is crucial for promoting energy efficiency and conservation measures, expanding hydroelectric power generation, enhancing domestic natural gas production and distribution, and encouraging research and development in alternative energy sources. By working together and sharing knowledge, engineers can drive the transformation towards a self-sufficient future for the United States, reducing our dependence on foreign oil imports and ensuring a sustainable energy future for generations to come.

Implications of breakthrough technologies for energy independence

In recent years, breakthrough technologies have emerged that offer tremendous potential for achieving energy independence in the United States. These advancements have the power to transform our energy landscape, reduce dependence on foreign oil imports, and pave the way for a self-sufficient future. In this subchapter, we will explore the implications of these breakthrough technologies and their significance in our quest for energy independence.

One area where breakthrough technologies are making a significant impact is in renewable energy strategies. The United States has vast resources of solar and wind energy, and developing domestic infrastructure to harness these sources is crucial. Advanced solar power technologies, such as photovoltaic cells and concentrated solar power systems, hold the promise of providing clean and abundant energy. Similarly, innovations in wind energy production and utilization, including more efficient turbines and improved grid integration, are enabling us to tap into the immense potential of wind power.

Biofuels are another area where breakthrough technologies are revolutionizing the energy sector. By investing in biofuel technologies, we can reduce our reliance on fossil fuels and promote the use of renewable resources. Advanced biofuel production methods, such as cellulosic ethanol and algae-based biofuels, offer higher energy yields and lower carbon emissions compared to conventional biofuels. These advancements not only contribute to energy independence but also help mitigate climate change.

Energy efficiency and conservation measures are also critical to achieving self-sufficiency in energy. Breakthrough technologies in this domain, such as smart grids, energy-efficient appliances, and building automation systems, enable us to optimize energy usage and reduce waste. By implementing these technologies, we can significantly decrease our energy consumption and reliance on external sources.

Nuclear power, often considered a controversial topic, has the potential to be a clean and reliable energy source. Advancements in nuclear reactor designs, such as small modular reactors and advanced fuel cycles, address concerns regarding safety and waste disposal. Expanding nuclear power generation can provide a stable and low-carbon energy option, complementing renewable sources.

Furthermore, breakthrough technologies can enhance domestic natural gas production and distribution. Advancements in hydraulic fracturing, or fracking, techniques have unlocked vast reserves of natural gas in the United States. By harnessing these resources, we can reduce dependence on foreign gas imports and transition to a more sustainable energy mix.

To maintain our position as a global leader in energy innovation, it is crucial to encourage research and development in alternative energy sources. Breakthrough technologies often stem from investment in research and collaboration between engineers, scientists, and policymakers. By fostering an environment that promotes innovation and supports clean energy research, we can continue to drive advancements in the energy sector.

In conclusion, breakthrough technologies offer immense implications for achieving energy independence in the United States. From developing domestic solar power infrastructure and increasing wind energy production to investing in biofuel technologies and advancing nuclear power, these advancements pave the way for a self-sufficient future. By embracing these technologies and implementing policies to reduce dependence on foreign oil imports, we can secure a sustainable and prosperous energy future for our nation.

Implementing policies to reduce dependence on foreign oil imports

One of the key challenges the United States faces in achieving energy independence is its heavy reliance on foreign oil imports. This subchapter will delve into various policies that can be implemented to reduce this dependence, offering engineers valuable strategies to work towards a more self-sufficient future.

To begin, it is essential to promote energy efficiency and conservation measures across all sectors. Engineers can play a critical role in designing and implementing innovative technologies and systems to reduce energy consumption. This includes developing more efficient transportation systems, improving building insulation, and encouraging the use of energy-saving appliances.

Investing in biofuel technologies is another effective strategy. Engineers can contribute by researching and developing advanced biofuel production methods, such as bioethanol and biodiesel, using sustainable feedstock. This not only reduces the need for imported oil but also helps mitigate greenhouse gas emissions.

Additionally, enhancing domestic natural gas production and distribution is crucial. Engineers can explore innovative drilling techniques, such as hydraulic fracturing, to tap into domestic natural gas reserves. Developing efficient transportation and storage infrastructure for natural gas will further strengthen the country's energy independence.

Advancing nuclear power as a clean energy source is another viable option. Engineers can focus on enhancing the safety, efficiency, and waste management of nuclear reactors. Additionally, investing in research and development for advanced reactor designs, such as small modular reactors, can contribute to reducing foreign oil imports.

Expanding hydroelectric power generation is yet another avenue for engineers to explore. By identifying suitable sites for new hydroelectric dams and optimizing existing facilities, engineers can harness the power of water to generate electricity, reducing the need for oil-based power generation.

Lastly, implementing effective policies to promote the use of renewable energy sources like solar and wind power is imperative. Engineers can contribute by developing domestic solar power infrastructure and increasing wind energy production and utilization. This involves designing and constructing efficient solar panels, wind turbines, and transmission systems that can seamlessly integrate renewable energy into the grid.

In conclusion, reducing dependence on foreign oil imports is a multifaceted challenge that requires a comprehensive approach. Engineers can play a pivotal role in this endeavor by implementing policies that focus on energy efficiency, investing in alternative energy sources, advancing nuclear power, expanding hydroelectric generation, and promoting renewable energy strategies. By collectively working towards these goals, the United States can pave the way for a self-sufficient future in energy.

Economic and national security implications of oil dependence

As engineers, we have a crucial role to play in shaping the future of energy independence in the United States. In this subchapter, we will discuss the economic and national security implications of our continued dependence on oil and the need for alternative strategies to achieve energy self-sufficiency.

Oil has been the lifeblood of our economy for decades, powering transportation, industry, and heating. However, this heavy reliance on oil leaves us vulnerable to price fluctuations in the global market and geopolitical tensions in oil-producing regions. The volatility of oil prices can have a cascading effect on our economy, causing inflation, job losses, and a decline in consumer spending. Moreover, our dependence on foreign oil imports threatens our national security by exposing us to supply disruptions and geopolitical risks.

To address these challenges, we must adopt a comprehensive approach that includes diverse strategies for energy self-sufficiency. One of the key elements of this strategy is the development of renewable energy sources. By investing in domestic solar power infrastructure, we can tap into the abundant solar energy resources across the country. Similarly, increasing wind energy production and utilization can provide a clean and reliable source of electricity, reducing our reliance on fossil fuels.

Another important aspect is the advancement of biofuel technologies. By investing in research and development, we can create sustainable and efficient biofuels that can replace petroleum-based fuels in transportation and other sectors. This not only reduces our dependence on oil but also helps mitigate climate change and reduce greenhouse gas emissions.

Energy efficiency and conservation measures also play a crucial role in reducing our oil dependence. By promoting energy-efficient technologies and practices, we can reduce energy waste and lower our overall energy consumption. This not only saves money for consumers and businesses but also reduces the need for oil-based energy sources.

Advancing nuclear power as a clean energy source is another avenue to explore. Nuclear power, when implemented safely and responsibly, can provide a stable and low-carbon source of electricity. Additionally, expanding hydroelectric power generation can harness the power of our rivers to generate clean electricity.

Enhancing domestic natural gas production and distribution can also contribute to reducing our reliance on oil. Natural gas is a cleaner-burning fuel compared to oil, and its abundant reserves within our borders provide an opportunity for energy independence.

Finally, it is crucial to encourage research and development in alternative energy sources. By investing in innovative technologies, we can unlock new ways to generate and store energy, paving the way for a sustainable and self-sufficient future.

In conclusion, our continued dependence on oil poses significant economic and national security risks. To achieve energy self-sufficiency, engineers must lead the way in developing a comprehensive strategy that includes renewable energy, biofuels, energy efficiency, nuclear power, hydroelectricity, natural gas, and alternative energy research. By implementing these strategies and reducing our dependence on foreign oil imports, we can create a more resilient and secure energy future for the United States.

The role of government in promoting energy independence

In the pursuit of a self-sufficient future, the role of government in promoting energy independence cannot be overstated. As engineers, it is imperative to understand the various strategies that the United States government can implement to achieve this goal. This subchapter aims to shed light on the crucial role of government in driving energy independence and the specific strategies that can be employed.

One of the primary strategies for the United States to become self-sufficient in energy is to develop renewable energy sources. The government can play a pivotal role in this by incentivizing and investing in renewable energy technologies such as solar power. By providing subsidies and tax benefits, the government can encourage the development of domestic solar power infrastructure, thereby reducing reliance on traditional energy sources.

Similarly, increasing wind energy production and utilization can also be a significant step towards energy independence. Government support in the form of grants and policies that facilitate the installation of wind farms can greatly contribute to the expansion of this renewable energy source.

Investing in biofuel technologies is another strategy that the government can adopt. By promoting research and development in this field and offering financial incentives to biofuel producers, the United States can decrease its dependence on fossil fuels and instead rely on domestically produced biofuels.

Furthermore, promoting energy efficiency and conservation measures is crucial. The government can implement policies that encourage energy-efficient practices in industries and households, such as enforcing building codes that promote energy conservation.

Advancing nuclear power as a clean energy source is also an essential aspect of promoting energy independence. The government can allocate funds for research and development of advanced nuclear technologies that are safer and more efficient, thus reducing reliance on conventional power plants.

Expanding hydroelectric power generation is another strategy that the government can adopt. By investing in the construction of new hydroelectric power plants and upgrading existing ones, the United States can tap into its abundant water resources to generate clean and renewable energy.

Enhancing domestic natural gas production and distribution is crucial for reducing dependence on foreign oil imports. The government can support the development of domestic natural gas reserves, invest in infrastructure for its extraction and distribution, and provide incentives for the use of natural gas as a cleaner alternative to other fossil fuels.

Lastly, the government can play a vital role in encouraging research and development in alternative energy sources. By allocating funds to universities and research institutions, the government can support the exploration of innovative technologies that can further diversify the energy mix and contribute to energy independence.

In conclusion, the role of government in promoting energy independence is pivotal. By implementing strategies such as developing domestic renewable energy sources, enhancing energy efficiency, and investing in alternative energy technologies, the government can lead the way towards a self-sufficient future. As engineers, it is our responsibility to collaborate with the government and contribute our expertise to achieve energy independence in the United States.

Strategies for reducing foreign oil imports

In this subchapter, we will explore various strategies that can be employed to reduce the United States' dependence on foreign oil imports. As engineers, it is our responsibility to develop and implement innovative solutions to ensure energy independence for our nation.

One of the key strategies is to invest in renewable energy sources. By developing domestic solar power infrastructure, we can harness the abundant sunlight available across the country. This will not only reduce our reliance on foreign oil but also contribute to a cleaner and more sustainable energy future. Similarly, increasing wind energy production and utilization will bolster our energy independence while also creating new job opportunities in the renewable energy sector.

Another promising avenue is investing in biofuel technologies. By promoting the research and development of advanced biofuels, we can reduce our dependence on fossil fuels and instead utilize domestically sourced biofuels. This will not only boost our energy independence but also support rural economies and reduce greenhouse gas emissions.

Energy efficiency and conservation measures play a crucial role in reducing oil imports. As engineers, we can design and implement energy-efficient technologies and systems in industries, transportation, and buildings. By optimizing energy consumption and reducing wastage, we can significantly decrease our reliance on foreign oil.

Advancing nuclear power as a clean energy source is another viable strategy. By investing in advanced nuclear technologies, we can ensure a reliable and carbon-free energy supply. Additionally, expanding hydroelectric power generation can provide a stable and renewable source of energy, further reducing our dependence on foreign oil.

Enhancing domestic natural gas production and distribution is essential. As engineers, we can develop innovative techniques for extracting natural gas while minimizing environmental impact. This will not only bolster our energy independence but also reduce greenhouse gas emissions compared to traditional fossil fuels.

Lastly, it is crucial to encourage research and development in alternative energy sources. By investing in innovative technologies such as hydrogen fuel cells, geothermal energy, and tidal power, we can diversify our energy portfolio and reduce our reliance on foreign oil imports.

Implementing policies to reduce dependence on foreign oil imports is essential. By advocating for renewable energy incentives, tax credits, and regulations that promote energy independence, engineers can drive significant change and help shape a self-sufficient energy future for the United States.

In conclusion, reducing foreign oil imports requires a multifaceted approach that leverages the expertise of engineers. By focusing on strategies such as developing renewable energy sources, promoting energy efficiency, advancing nuclear power, and enhancing domestic production of natural gas, we can pave the way for a self-sufficient energy future in the United States.

Balancing environmental concerns with oil production and consumption

In our pursuit of energy independence, it is crucial to address the pressing issue of balancing environmental concerns with oil production and consumption. As engineers, we play a vital role in developing strategies that not only meet our energy needs but also minimize the negative impact on the environment.

One of the key ways to achieve this balance is by investing in renewable energy strategies for the United States. By shifting our focus towards cleaner and sustainable sources of energy, such as solar and wind power, we can reduce our reliance on oil and decrease carbon emissions. Developing domestic solar power infrastructure and increasing wind energy production and utilization are particularly important steps in this direction.

Furthermore, investing in biofuel technologies can also contribute to a more sustainable energy future. Biofuels, derived from organic matter, offer a renewable alternative to fossil fuels. By supporting research and development in this field, engineers can help optimize biofuel production processes and make them more economically viable.

Another area that warrants our attention is energy efficiency and conservation measures. By promoting energy-efficient practices and technologies, we can significantly reduce our overall energy consumption. This not only helps in minimizing our dependence on oil but also lowers greenhouse gas emissions and saves costs for consumers.

Advancing nuclear power as a clean energy source is another avenue worth exploring. Nuclear energy has the potential to provide a significant amount of power while emitting virtually no carbon dioxide. However, it is crucial to ensure the safe and responsible management of nuclear waste and invest in research to develop even more efficient and secure nuclear technologies.

In addition to these renewable options, we must also consider expanding hydroelectric power generation and enhancing domestic natural gas production and distribution. These sources can act as transitional fuels towards a more sustainable energy future.

Finally, implementing policies to reduce dependence on foreign oil imports is crucial for achieving energy independence. By prioritizing domestic production and incentivizing research and development in alternative energy sources, we can reduce our reliance on volatile global oil markets and enhance national security.

In conclusion, balancing environmental concerns with oil production and consumption is a complex challenge that requires the collective efforts of engineers and policymakers. By embracing strategies such as investing in renewable energy, promoting energy efficiency, and reducing dependence on foreign oil, we can pave the way towards a self-sufficient and environmentally responsible energy future for the United States.